MongoDB

Learn MongoDB in a simple way!

By Dan Warnock

Table of Contents

Introduction   5

Chapter 1- An overview of MongoDB   6

Chapter 2- Deploying a Replica Set   7

Chapter 3- Adding members to a Replica Set   14

Chapter 4- Removal of a Member from a Replica Set   23

Chapter 5- Replacing a Replica Set Member   30

Chapter 6- Setting the Priority for a Member   31

Chapter 7- Changing the Oplog Size   35

Chapter 8- Common Database Commands   44

Chapter 9- Data Recovery   47

Chapter 10- Analyzing the Performance of Database
Operations   56

Chapter 11- Rotating Log Files   69

Chapter 12- Backup and Restore   76

Conclusion   86

Disclaimer

While all attempts have been made to verify the information provided in this book, the author does assume any responsibility for errors, omissions, or contrary interpretations of the subject matter contained within. The information provided in this book is for educational and entertainment purposes only. The reader is responsible for his or her own actions and the author does not accept any responsibilities for any liabilities or damages, real or perceived, resulting from the use of this information.

The trademarks that are used are without any consent, and the publication of the trademark is without permission or backing by the trademark owner. All trademarks and brands within this book are for clarifying purposes only and are the owned by the owners themselves, not affiliated with this document.

Introduction

MongoDB is a very powerful NoSQL database in terms of performance and the operations that it can support. It is good for both database developers and programmers. Programmers can link their MongoDB database with the various programming languages. This book helps you to learn MongoDB.

Chapter 1- An overview of MongoDB

The MongoDB database was written in C++. It is among the leading NoSQL databases today. One can achieve a lot in terms of a database with MongoDB. The database offers automatic scaling, high performance, and high availability to database developers.

Chapter 2- Deploying a Replica Set

We need to discuss the process by which one can create a three-member replica set from three MongoDB existing instances which are executed with access control already disabled.

When you have three member replica sets, you will ensure that there is enough redundancy for enabling us to survive failures such as network partitions. They will also provide us with enough capacity to cater to the distributed read operations. The number of members in the replica sets should always be an odd number. This ensures that the elections are done smoothly.

You just have to start the MongoDB instances that are to become members of the replica set, perform a configuration of the replica set, and then have the instances of the MongoDB added to it.

For production deployments, the instances of MongoDB have to be stored in different machines so as to ensure that there is much separation between the members. For those using virtual machines for production deployments, each instance of the MongoDB has to be placed in different host servers serviced by redundant network paths and redundant power circuits.

The procedure

The following steps are necessary for deployment of a replica set when the access control has been disabled:

1. Use the appropriate options to start each member of your replica set

   A mongod should be started for each member and the name of the replica set specified through the option for "*replSet.*" For applications connecting to more than one replica set, a distinct name should be specified for each set.

   Let us use the option "replSet" to specify the name of our replica set:

mongod --replSet "rso"

The specification for this can also be done in the configuration file. For the mongod to be started together with the configuration file, we can use the "—config" option so as to specify this:

mongod --config $HOME/.mongodb/config

In production deployments, an "*init script*" can be configured for management of this process.

2. Connection of the mongo shell to the replica set member

Assuming that you have your mongod running on localhost and on the port 27017, which is the default one, you can use the following:

Mongo

3. Initiation of the replica set

One should use the function *"rs.initiate()"* on their replica set member. This is shown below:

rs.initiate()

MongoDB will initiate a set having the current member, and it will use the default configuration for the replica set.

4. Verifying the initial configuration of the replica set

The displaying of the replica set configuration object can be done by use of the method *"rs.conf()."* The configuration object for the replica set is as follows:

{

```
"_id" : "rso",

"version" : 1,

"members" : [

    {

        "_id" : 1,

        "host" : "mongodb0.example.net:27017"

    }

]

}
```

5. The remaining members should then be added to the replica set.

    This can be done by use of the method *"rs.add()."* Consider the following example, which shows how two members can be added:

```
rs.add("mongodb0.example.net")
rs.add("mongodb1.example.net")
```

After completion, you will have a fully functional replica set. It will then elect the primary.

6. The status of the replica set can then be checked. The following method can be used to perform this operation:

rs.status()

Chapter 3- Adding members to a Replica Set

An additional member can be added to a replica set which is already in existence. Note that each replica set should have a maximum of seven voting members. For one to add a new member to a replica set which has seven members, you have to add the new member as a non-voting member or remove a vote from one of the existing members.

In the case of production deployments, an *"init script"* can be configured for the purpose of management of the member processes.

A member who has been removed from the replica set can be re-added. If the removal of the member had been done recently, the member can be recovered and catch up easily.

For those having a snapshot or a backup of an existing member, the data files can be moved to a new system and then quickly used for initiation of a new member. The files have to be:

1. A copy of data files which are valid for a member belonging to the same replica set.

2. The most recent operation in the primary's oplog. The new member has to become the current one once the operations from the primary's oplog have been applied.

Requirements

You should have the following:

1. A replica set which is active.

2. A new MongoDB system with the ability to support your
    data set, and be accessible by your active replica set
    throughout your network.

The Procedure

1. Preparation of the Directory

Before we can add the new member to the replica set, we have to prepare the data directory for the new members. You can use any one of the following strategies:

- Make sure that the data directory for new members has no data. Data will be copied from an existing member by the new member. For a new member in a recovering state, it has to exit and then become a secondary before all the data can be copied by MongoDB as part of the replication process. Note that some time will be required for this process to take place, but the administrator will not be required to intervene in any way.

- The data directory has to be copied manually from the existing member. The new member will become a secondary member, and it will catch up to the current state of our replica set. When we copy the data, the amount of time required for the new member to become the current one will be shortened.

Ensure that you are in a position to copy the data directory to the new member, and then begin the replication within the window which is allowed by the oplog. Otherwise, an initial sync will have to be performed by the new instance, and the data will be completely resynchronized.

2. Addition of a New Member to an Existing Replica Set

    1. Begin by launching an instance of the MongoDB. You can then specify the replica set name and the data directory. Consider the example given below:

mongod --dbpath /suf/mongodb/dbo --replSet rso

In the above example, we have specified both the replica set and the data directory. The host name and the information about the port for the new instance of MongoDB also has to be specified.

Also, the replica set and the data directory can be specified in the configuration file *"mongod.conf,"* and then the following command used to start the instance of mongod:

mongod --config /etc/mongod.conf

2. Establish a connection to the primary of the replica set

Members can only be added once you have established a connection to the primary. If you are not aware of the primary member of the replica set, log in to any of the members of the replica set and then execute the following command:

db.isMaster()

3. The method "*rs.add()*" can then be used for addition of a new member to the replica set. Consider the example given below:

rs.add("mongodb3.mydb.net")

In the above example, we are adding a new member to the host "*mongodb3.mydb.net.*" You can also specify the port number depending on the setup that you are using as shown below:

rs.add("mongodb3.mydb.net:27017")

4. You can then verify to check whether the member has been added to the replica set. This can be done using the following method so as to display the configuration of the replica set:

rs.conf()

To view the status of your replica set, use the following method:

rs.status()

Configuration and Addition of a New Member

To add a new member to the replica set, you just have to pass the member document to the method "*rs.add()*." Consider a situation in which we want to add a member with the following information to the replica set:

- an _id of 1.

- A port number and hostname of mongodb3.mydb.net:27017.

- a priority value within our replica set of 0.

- a configuration as hidden

The following command can be used for adding the above member:

```
rs.add({_id: 1, host: "mongodb3.mydb.net:27017", priority: 0, hidden: true})
```

Chapter 4- Removal of a Member from a Replica Set

In MongoDB, it is possible for us to remove a member from a replica set. There are different procedures which can be used to do this. Let us discuss these methods.

Using rs.remove()

1. Begin by shutting down the MongoDB instance of the user that you are in need of removing from the replica set. To do this, you just have to establish a connection using the mongo shell, and then execute the method *"db.shutdownServer()."*

2. Establish a connection with the current primary of the replica set. To know your current primary, execute the method *"db.isMaster()"* after establishment of a connection with any member in the replica set.

3. The member can then be removed using the method *"rs.remove()."* There are two forms that can be used to do this:

rs.remove("mongod3.mydb.net:27017")

rs.remove("mongod3.mydb.net")

The shell will be briefly disconnected by the MongoDB as the replica set continues to elect the new primary. It will then be reconnected automatically. Note that even if the command succeeds, the shell will have to display the error *"DBClientCursor::init call() failed."*

Using rs.reconfig()

One can remove a member from the replica set by editing the replica set configuration document as describe below:

1. Begin by shutting down the instance of the mongod for the member you want to remove from the replica set. Once you have used the mongo shell to connect, execute the method _"db.shutdownServer()"_ so as to shut down.

2. Establish a connection to the current primary of the replica set. If you are not aware of the primary, connect to any member of the replica set and then execute the method _"db.isMaster()."_

3. View the current document with the configuration details by executing the method _"rs.conf(),"_ and then determine from the array the position of the members

that you want to remove. Consider the example configuration document given below:

```
{
  "_id" : "rs",
  "version" : 7,
  "members" : [
    {
      "_id" : 0,
      "host" : "mongod_A.mydb.net:27017"
    },
    {
      "_id" : 1,
      "host" : "mongod_B.mydb.net:27017"
    },
    {
      "_id" : 2,
      "host" : "mongod_C.mydb.net:27017"
    }
```

]

4. The current configuration document can then be assigned to the variable "*cfg*" as shown below:

cfg = rs.conf()

5. Remove the member by modifying the object "*cfg.*" Suppose you need to remove "mongod_C.mydb.net:27017," use the following JavaScript operation:

cfg.members.splice(2,1)

6. You can then overwrite the configuration document of the replica set by issuing the following command:

rs.reconfig(cfg)

After executing the above command, the replica set will be disconnected as the negotiation for the new primary is being done. After that, the reconnection will be done automatically. Even after the operation runs successfully, the error *"DBClientCursor::init call() failed"* will be displayed so you don't have to worry about this.

7. You can then confirm the new configuration by executing the command *"rs.conf()."* In my case, I get the following:

```
{
    "_id" : "rs",
    "version" : 8,
    "members" : [
        {
            "_id" : 0,
            "host" : "mongod_A.mydb.net:27017"
        },
        {
            "_id" : 1,
            "host" : "mongod_B.mydb.net:27017"
        }
    ]
}
```

Chapter 5- Replacing a Replica Set Member

It is possible for one to change the name of the host of a member of the replica set without having to change the configuration of the set or the member.

For the hostname of a replica set to be changed, the *"host"* field has to be modified. The value of the field *"_id"* will not be changed even after reconfiguring the set.

For the name of the host to be changed to *"mongo2.mydb.net,"* for our replica set member which has been configured at index 0, we can do the following:

cfg = rs.conf()

cfg.members[0].host = "mongo2.mydb.net"

rs.reconfig(cfg)

Chapter 6- Setting the Priority for a Member

This is responsible for determining the outcome of the election of the primary. It is mostly used to influence this election in which some members are made to be more likely to become the primary. The priority is set in the form of a number, and the one having a higher number is more likely to become the primary.

Considerations

For the priorities to be modified, the members array contained in the replica configuration object has to be updated. The index of the array begins at 0. The value of the array index should not be confused with the member's_id field of the replica set in the replica set. The value for the priority has to range between 0 and 1000, and it can take a floating point number. Its default value is 1.

When a particular member is assigned a priority of 0, it will not be considered during the election of the primary.

The adjustment of a priority should only be done during a scheduled maintenance period. When this value has been reconfigured, it can force the current primary to be dropped, and then an election sought. Before an election is carried out, all of the client connections which are open are closed by the primary.

Procedure

1. Copy the configuration of the replica set to a variable.

   In the mongo shell, retrieve the configuration of the replica set by executing the function "rs.conf()" and then assign it to a variable.An example is given below:

cfg = rs.conf()

2. Change the priority value of each member.

   This should be changed as the configuration has been done in the array having the members. Consider the example given below:

cfg.members[0].priority = 3

cfg.members[1].priority = 2

cfg.members[2].priority = 2

With the configuration, the priority value for the first three members of the array will be changed.

3. The replica set should then be set to the new configuration.

The new configuration can be set by using the method "*rs.reconfig()*." This is shown below:

rs.reconfig(cfg)

With the above command, the configuration of the replica set will be updated using the value of the configuration defined in the variable "*cfg*."

Chapter 7- Changing the Oplog Size

The oplog is found internally as a capped collection, meaning that its size cannot be modified during the normal operations. The size of the oplog needed is variable due to some circumstances.

For this to be changed, one has to perform maintenance on the members of the replica set in turn. This should involve stopping the instance of the MongoDB, and then starting a standalone instance of it, modifying the size of the oplog, and then restarting the member.

Procedure

1. The member should be restarted in standalone mode.

    The method "*rs.stepDown()*" should be forced to make a primary become a secondary.

2. The oplog should then be recreated with a new size, and an old oplog entry should be used as the seed.

3. The MongoDB instance should then be restarted as a member of our replica set.

Restarting a Secondary in a Standalone Mode on a Different Port

Identify any one of the non-primary members of the mongod instance in your replica set, and then shut it down. Use the command

"_db.shutdownServer()_" as shown below:

db.shutdownServer()

The mongod instance should then be restarted as a standalone instance executing on a different port and without the parameter "—REPLSET." A command similar to the one given below should be used:

mongod --port 37017 --dbpath /mydb/mongodb

Creation of a Backup of Oplog

Note that this is optional. The existing oplog should be backed up on a standalone instance as shown below:

mongodump --db local --collection 'oplog.rs' --port 37017

Recreating the oplog having a new Seed Entry and Size

Begin by saving the last entry from your oplog. You can use the mongo shell to connect to the instance, and then switch to the local database by executing the following command:

use local

The db object can be set by use of the operation given below:

db = db.getSiblingDB('local')

The temp temporary collection should be empty, and this is why we have to drop the collection as shown below:

db.temp.drop()

You should then find the last entry, and then save it in a temporary collection by use of the method *"db.collection.save()"* and a resort on the reverse natural order. This is shown below:

database.temp.save(database.oplog.rs.find({ }, { ts: 1, h: 1 }).sort({$natural : -1}).limit(1).next())

The oplog enetry can be viewed using the following operation:

db.temp.find()

Removing the Oplog Collection in Existence

The old collection, that is, "oplog.rs," should be removed from the local database. To do this, use the following commands:

db = db.getSiblingDB('local')

db.oplog.rs.drop()

After the above commands, a _"true"_ will be returned to the shell.

Creating a New Oplog

This can be done by use of the command *"create,"* and a new oplog of a new size will be created. The size argument has to be specified in bytes. To create an oplog worth 2 gigabytes, the specification should be 2 * 1024 * 1024 * 1024. This is shown in the command given below:

database.runCommand({ create: "oplog.rs", capped: true, size: (2 * 1024 * 1024 * 1024) })

If the above command runs successfully, you will get the following return:

{ "ok" : 1 }

Insertion into the New Oplog

The last entry which was saved previously in the old oplog can be inserted into the new oplog. An example of this is given below:

database.oplog.rs.save(database.temp.findOne())

The following command can be used for confirming whether the entry has been inserted into the new oplog:

db.oplog.rs.find()

Restarting the Member

The mongod should be restarted as a member of our replica set on its normal port. An example of this is given below:

db.shutdownServer()

mongod --replSet rso --dbpath /mydb/mongodb

The member of the replica set will then recover and catch up before it can become eligible for election as the primary.

This procedure should then be repeated for all of the members for whom you havethe need of changing their oplog. It should also be repeated for the size of the oplog on the primary. The method "_rs.stepDown()_" should be used for this.

Chapter 8- Common Database Commands

With the command interface for MongoDB, one can access all of the non CRUDE operations. With the commands, one can accomplish various tasks such as initialization of a replica set, fetching of server statistics, and others.

For us to specify a command, we have to begin by constructing a standard BSON document, and the first key should be the name of the command. A good example of this is the *"isMaster"* command which can be specified by using the following BSON document:

{ isMaster: 1 }

Issuing Commands

With the mongo shell, a helper method named "*db.runCommand()*," which can help us to run commands. Consider the operation given below which can be used for running the above command:

db.runCommand({ isMaster: 1 })

admin Database Commands

Some commands have to be executed on the admin database. The commands will always look as follows:

use admin

db.runCommand({buildInfo: 1})

However, there is a helper which executes the command automatically once in the admin database. This is shown below:

db._adminCommand({buildInfo: 1})

Whenever any of the MongoDB commands has executed successfully, it returns a status value of 1 as shown below:

{ 'ok': 1 }

When a command has failed, it will return an ok message with a status value of 0.

Chapter 9- Data Recovery

Sometimes, the system might be shut down unexpectedly. In that case, the data on the data will be left in an inconsistent state. For data consistency to be maintained, the database has to be shut down in a clean manner. The durability journaling should also be used. With MongoDB, data is written to the journal after every 100 milliseconds, and this makes it possible to recover the database even in cases of an unclean shutdown.

If the execution of the instance is not done as part of the replica set, and journaling has not been enabled, the following procedure can be used for the purpose of recovering data which is in an inconsistent state. In case the execution is done as part of the replica set, the restoration should be done from a backup or the instance of the mongod restarted with an empty dbpath and then allow the MongoDB to do an initial sync so as to restore the data.

The following methods can be used to ensure a clean shutdown of MongoDB:

- The init script of the system.

- The option "MONGOD –SHUTDOWN" IN MONGODB.

- CONTROL-C WHEN THE EXECUTION OF MONGODB IS DONE IN INTERACTIVE MODE.

- METHOD "*db.shutdownServer()*" on the Mongo shell.

Process Indication

If you are aware of any instance of MongoDB which is running without journaling, and then it stops unexpectedly and you were not using replication, then you have to run the repair operation before you can start the MongoDB. If you were using replication during the shutdown, then you just have to restore the database from a backup and then allow the replication to carry out an initial sync for the data to be restored.

Note that the file named "mongod.lock" in the directory "/data/db" is not of size 0 bytes, then your MongoDB will fail to start. If this is the case, then the following error message will be found in the file:

Unclean shutdown detected.

Once you see the above error, just know that you have to run the MongoDB by use of the "−REPAIR" OPTION. IF THE

FILE "mongodb.lock" exists on the system and then you open the database with the above option, or with the optional "—REPAIRPATH," A MESSAGE WITH THE FOLLOWING LINE WILL BE OBSERVED:

old lock file: /data/db/mongod.lock. probably means unclean shutdown

In case you observe the above message, you can go ahead and remove the lockfile, and then execute the repair operation before the database can be opened normally.

When your system suffers from an unexpected shutdown, then there are two ways on how data files can be repaired, which include the following:

- Use of the option "—REPAIR" TOGETHER WITH THE OPTION "—REPAIRPATH." THE MONGODB WILL THEN READ YOUR DATA FILES WHICH ARE EXISTING, AND THE DATA FOUND WILL BE WRITTEN TO THE AVAILABLE DATA FILES.

BEFORE YOU CAN USE THIS PROCEDURE, YOU WILL NOT BE REQUIRED TO REMOVE THE FILE "*mongod.lock.*"

- By use of the "−REPAIR" OPTION. THE MONGOD WILL HAVE TO READ THE DATA FROM THE EXISTING FILES, AND THEN THIS DATA WILL BE WRITTEN TO NEW FILES, AND THE FILES IN EXISTENCE WHICH ARE CORRUPT WILL BE REPLACED WITH THE NEW FILES. THE FILE "mongod.lock" has to be removed before this procedure can be used.

The following procedure can be used for repairing the data files and then preserving the original ones.

For the data files to be repaired by use of the "−REPAIRPATH" OPTION, AND FOR THE ORIGINAL DATA FILES TO BE PRESERVED, THE FOLLOWING STEPS ARE NECESSARY:

1. USE THE OPTION TO START THE MONGOD FOR THE ORIGINAL FILES TO BE REPLACED WITH THE REPAIRED ONES. USE THE OPTIONS "—REPAIR" AND "—REPAIRPATH" TO START THE MONGODB. A COMMAND SIMILAR TO THE ONE GIVEN BELOW SHOULD BE ISSUED:

    mongod --dbpath /data/mydb --repair --repairpath /data/dbo

    Once the process has completed, the data files which have been repaired will be placed in the directory *"/data/dbo."*

2. The MongoDB instance should then be started with the new data directory

    The mongodb instance should be started with the dbPath pointed to "/data/dbo." This is shown below:

mongod --dbpath /data/dbo

Once you have confirmed and found that the new data files are fully operational, the old ones can be deleted or archived in the directory "/data/db." The files which have been repaired can also be moved to the old database or the dbpath updated so as to point to the new location.

Repair of Data Files without Preservation of the Old Files

If we are not in need of preserving the old files during the repair of the data files, we do not have to use the option "—REPAIRPATH." THE FOLLOWING STEPS CAN BE FOLLOWED:

1. Begin by removing the stale lock file.

   An example of how this can be done is shown below:

rm /data/mydb/mongod.lock

   The directory "/data/mydb" has to be replaced with the dbpath in which your MongoDB original data files are located.

2. The MongoDB instance should then be started with the option for replacing the original files with the

repaired ones. The option "—REPAIR" SHOULD BE USED FOR THIS, AND THE ORIGINAL FILES WILL BE REPLACED WITH THE REPAIRED ONES. A COMMAND WHICH IS SIMILAR TO THE ONE GIVEN BELOW SHOULD BE ISSUED:

mongod --dbpath /data/mydb —repair

Once the execution of the above command has been completed, the original files contained in the directory *"/data/db"* will be replaced by the new files.

3. Start the MongoDB normally

The following command, which points to our dbPath *"/data/mydb"* should be used for this purpose:

mongod --dbpath /data/mydb

Chapter 10- Analyzing the Performance of Database Operations

With the database profiler, fine grained data can be collected, and this is always in terms of write operations, database commands, and commands which are running on the instance of the MongoDB. The profiling can be enabled in terms of either per-database or per-instance. During the process of enabling profiling, we can also configure the profiling level.

Once the database has collected data, it writes all of it to the collection *"system.profile,"* which is just a capped collection.

The following are some of the available profiling levels in MongoDB:

- 0- The profiler is off and no data will be collected.

- 1- Only data for the slow operations will be collected. The default setting for slow operations are the ones which are below 100 milliseconds.

- 2- This will collect all the profiling data for the database operations.

The process of enabling data profiling can be done from the Mongo shell or through a driver which makes use of the *"profile"* command. We will guide you on how to do this via the Mongo shell.

When you have enabled the process of profiling, the profiling level will also be set. The data about the profiling will be recorded in the collection named *"system.profile."*

For one to enable profiling and then set the profiling level, the method *"db.setProfilingLevel()"* should be used. This should be done in the mongo shell, and the parameter passed should be the profiling level.

An example is when you need to set or enable profiling for all of your database operations. This can be done as shown below:

db.setProfilingLevel(2)

After that, the shell will give you a document which shows your previous profiling level. The value 1 and the *"ok"* are an indication that your command executed successfully. This is shown below:

{ "was" : 0, "slowms" : 100, "ok" : 1 }

Threshold for Slow Connections

When it comes to slow connections, the threshold will apply to all of your database operations. When this has been changed, it is changed for all of the databases in the instance.

Slow thresholds are usually below 100 milliseconds. If your database has a profiling level of 1, operations which are slower than 100 milliseconds will be logged.

For the threshold to be set, two parameters have to be passed to the helper *"db.setProfilingLevel()"* in the mongo shell. The first parameter will be responsible for setting the profiling level for the current database, and the second one will set it for the slow operation and then used as the default level.

Consider the command given below which will set the profiling level to 0, and this will disable the profiling. The slow operation threshold will also be set to 20 milliseconds. A database which is on an instance of 1 will then use this threshold. The command is given below:

db.setProfilingLevel(0,20)

Sometimes, you might want to check your profiling level.

This can be done on the mongo shell by executing the following command:

db.getProfilingStatus()

Once the above command has been executed, the shell will give you the following result:

{ "was" : 0, "slowms" : 100 }

The field *"was"* gives us the current profiling level. The field *"slowms"* will tell us about how long an operation will exist for it to pass the *"slow"* threshold, and this is specified in terms of milliseconds.

If you need to return only the profiling level, the helper *"db.getProfilingLevel()"* should be used. This is shown below:

db.getProfilingLevel()

Disabling profiling

Profiling can be disabled by executing the following command in the mongo shell:

db.setProfilingLevel(0)

The profiling can also be enabled for an entire instance of MongoDB. This is usually the case in development environments, and it facilitates the testing process. The profiling level will apply to all the databases which have been provided by the instance of MongoDB.

For profiling to be enabled for an instance of MongoDB, the following parameters should be passed to mongod during startup or in the configuration file:

mongod --profile=1 --slowms=15

With the above parameters, the profiling level will be set to 1, meaning that only data for slow connections will be collected, and slow operations are the ones which will be executed for more than 15 milliseconds.

It is not possible for one to enable profiling for an instance of mongos. For you to be able to enable profiling for a shard cluster, it has to be first enabled for each instance of mongod in the cluster.

The data for the profiler can also be viewed. The collection *"system.profile"* provides us with the database profiler logs, and this is all about our operations. For the profiling information to be viewed, one has to query the above collection. One can also use "$comment" for adding data to the query document and the process of analyzing data from the profiler will be made much easier.

We need to give some examples of profiler data queries.

Suppose you need to get the 20 most recent log entries into the collection, a query similar to the one given below can be executed:

db.system.profile.find().limit(20).sort({ ts : -1 }).pretty()

For the purpose of returning all of the operations except the "*$cmd*", that is, command operations, a query similar to the one given below can be executed:

db.system.profile.find({ op: { $ne : 'command' } }).pretty()

Operations associated with a certain collection can be returned by use of the query given below:

db.system.profile.find({ ns : 'db1.collection1' }).pretty()

With the above query, we need to return the operations on the database "*db*" specifically in the collection "*collection1.*"

The following query can be executed to get the operations which are slower than 10 milliseconds:

db.system.profile.find({ millis : { $gt : 10 } }).pretty()

If you are in need of obtaining information about operations which took place in a certain range of time, execute the query shown below:

db.system.profile.find(

        {

       ts : {

          $gt : new ISODate("2015-10-09T04:00:00Z") ,

          $lt : new ISODate("2015-12-20T03:40:00Z")

        }

       }

).pretty()

That is how simply we can do it.

With the example given below, we will look at the time range, suppress the user field from the output so as to make it easier for reading, and then the results are sorted based on the time taken to execute. Here is the example:

db.system.profile.find(

      {

     ts : {

       $gt : new ISODate("2014-07-15T04:00:00Z") ,

       $lt : new ISODate("2015-07-12T05:30:00Z")

      }

    },

    { user : 0 }

).sort({ millis : -1 })

When you enable profiling in your database, once you execute the helper *"show profile"* on the mongo shell, you will get the 5 most recent operations which have taken at least 1 millisecond to be executed. You have to issue the command "show profile" on the mongo shell as we have shown it below:

show profile

Once profiling has been enabled, it will have an effect, though minor on the performance of the system. The collection *"system.profile"* is a capped collection having a default size of 1 gigabyte. With storage of this size, one can store several profiling documents. The amount of profiling data used for an operation is different in various applications.

Changing the size of the collection "system.profile" on the profile

The size of the above collection can be changed by following the steps given below:

1. Begin by disabling profiling.

2. Drop the collection *"system.profile."*

3. Create a new collection for *"system.collection."*

4. You can then re-enable the profiling.

If you need to create this collection with a size of 3,000,000 bytes, the following sequence of commands can be used on the mongo shell:

db.setProfilingLevel(0)

db.system.profile.drop()

db.createCollection("system.profile", { capped: true, size:3000000 })

db.setProfilingLevel(1)

Chapter 11- Rotating Log Files

When you use the option "--LOGPATH" or with the setting "systemLog.path," the mongos and the mongod instances will report all of the activity and operations and then record them in a log file. This will be done live. When the reporting to the log file is being done, what happens is that the MongoDB will rotate the logfile in response to the command *"logRotate"* or after the mongos or mongod has received a signal of type SIGUSR1 from the operating system.

The standard MongoDB log rotation process will archive the current log file and then start a new one. The mongos or mongod will rename the current logfile by appending a UTC timestamp to the name of the file, and this is done in ISODate format. A new log file will be opened, the old log file closed, and all of the new log entries will be sent to your new log file.

We need to demonstrate how the default log rotation takes place in MongoDB. This can be done as follows:

1. Start an instance of MongoDB.

This can be done as shown below:

mongod -v --logpath /var/log/mongodb/myserver.log

2. Listing log files.

Use a separate terminal, and then list the matching files as follows:

ls /var/log/mongodb/myserver.log*

3. Rotate the log files.

This can be done by issuing the command "*logRotate*" in the mongo shell. It should also be from the admin database. This is shown below:

use admin

db.runCommand({ logRotate : 1 })

4.   View the created log files.

You can now view the log files which have been newly created. The command given below can be used for this purpose:

ls /var/log/mongodb/myserver.log*

Two log files should be listed, that is, "*server1.log*" and "*server1.log.<timestamp>*." The latter is the renamed log file, while the former is the log file created by mongos or mongod after it reopened the log file. When log files have been rotated, the old ones which have been rotated are not modified. A timestamp has to be added to the log file which is to be rotated.

Using "--logRotate reopen" to rotate the Log

With this, the log file will be closed and then reopened by use of the typical log rotation behavior of Linux/Unix. The following steps can be followed:

1. Start an instance of mongod and use the reopen behavior of "**--LOGROTATE.** "

   The command given below can be used:

mongod -v --logpath /var/log/mongodb/myserver.log --logRotate reopen –logappend

   Note that the option "--LOGAPPEND" has to be used with the "--LOGROTATE REOPEN."

2. List your log files.

Use a separate terminal, and then list the matching files by use of the command given below:

ls /var/log/mongodb/myserver.log*

The result has to have one log file, which is *"myserver.log."*

3. Rotate the log file.

Use the *"logRotate"* command so as to rotate the log file on the mongo shell and from the admin database. This is shown below:

use admin

db.runCommand({ logRotate : 1 })

An external process should be used for renaming the log file, following the typical log rotation behavior used in Linux/Unix.

Syslog Log Rotation

With this process, the log data is send to the syslog by MongoDB but it is not written to a file. The following steps are necessary:

1. Use the "**--SYSLOG** " option to start an instance of mongod.

   This is shown below:

mongod —syslog

The "—logpath" should not be included. This is because it will lead to an error as the option "—syslog" will tell the mongod to send the data to the syslog. In case you are in need of specifying the facility level to be used when logging messages to our syslog, the option "--SYSLOGFACILITY," or the configuration setting "systemLog.syslogFacility."

2.   Rotate the log.

Use the default log rotation mechanism of your system so as to store and rotate the log output.

It is also possible for one to use "SIGUSR1" so as to force a log rotation to take place. This is shown below:

kill -SIGUSR1 <mongod process id>

Chapter 12- Backup and Restore

There are some utilities provided together with MongoDB which can be used for performing the process of backup and restoration of data. Note that these tools and utilities perform an interaction with the instance of MongoDB which is in execution, meaning that it can impact the performance of your database. They have the impact of creating traffic for the database which is running, and forcing it to read all of its data through the memory. When infrequently used data is read by MongoDB, the more frequently used data can be supplanted, and this will have an effect of deteriorating the performance of the regular workload for the database.

Use of mongodump for Backup

With this tool, the contents of the local database will not be dumped. For all of the databases to be backed up via the mongodump, one should hae the _"backup"_ role. This role will provide you with all the roles which are required for backing up the data.

For you to backup a particular database, you must have read access on it. There are several roles which can provide you with this access, and this will include the _"backup"_ role.

For the collection _"systemprofile"_ to be backed up, whose creation is after activation of database profiling, one must be having an additional read access on the collection. There are several roles which can provide you with this access.

For one to backup the users and the user-defined roles, they must have a read access on the admin database. This is because in MongoDB, all the information regarding the users and their roles is stored in the admin database.

Consider a situation in which you want to backup data from an instance of mongos or MongoDB. This is running on the same machine and on the default port, which is 27017. The following command can be used for this purpose:

Mongodump

Mongodump version 2.2 and above uses a data format which is incompatible with the earlier versions of the mongod. Recent versions of mongodump should not be used for backing up the older versions of data stores.

The host and the port of the instance of MongoDB which the mongodump is to connect to can also be specified. An example of this is given below:

mongodump --host mongodb.mydb.net --port 27017

Consider the example given below, which shows how a different output directory can be specified:

mongodump --out /data/backup/

For you to limit the amount of data which has been included in the database dump, the options --DB and –COLLECTION CAN BE SPECIFIED IN THE MONGODUMP. AN EXAMPLE OF THIS IS GIVEN BELOW:

mongodump --collection collection1 --db mydb

The above command will create a dump of a collection, and give it the name *"collection."* This will be done from the database named *"mydb"* located in the *"dump/"* subdirectory of our current working directory.

In case output files are found in the backup data folder, then mongodump will overwrite them. Before executing the mongodump command severally, you should ensure that the files you are having in the output folder are not needed anymore. Alternatives, the folders or the files can be renamed. It is also possible for us to create backups from non-local instances of mongod. This is accomplished by specifying the "*host*" and "*port*" options for the command "*mongodump*" which will help in backing up data contained in a remote host. Consider the example given below, which shows how this can be accomplished:

mongodump --host mongodb.mydb.net --port 3017 --username user --password pass --out /opt/backup/mongodump-2015-11-16

Mongostore

This is used for restoring a Mongo database. However, for the restoration of the database to be done, the user has to have a read/write access on each of the databases which is to be restored. For the users and user-defined roles to be restored, one has to have access to the admin database.

When you want to use this tool so as to establish a connection to an active mongos or mongod, a command with the following prototype form should be used:

mongorestore --port <port number> <path to the backup>

Consider the example given below:

mongorestore dump-2015-09-17/

In the above case, the MongoDB will import the database backup from the directory 2015-09-17 to the instance of mongod which is running on the local interface.

In case you had used the option "−*oplog*" to create your database so as to make sure there is a point-in-time snapshot, then use the option "−OPLOGREPLAY" SO AS TO CALL THE MONGOSTORE. THIS IS SHOWN IN THE EXAMPLE GIVEN BELOW:

mongorestore −oplogReplay

That is how it can be done.

During the insertion of items into the database, one can use the option "MONGORESTORE −OBJCHECK" SO AS TO CHECK ON THE INTEGRITY OF THESE ITEMS. THE OPTION "MONGORESTORE −DROP" MAY ALSO BE USED FOR DROPPING EACH COLLECTION FROM THE

DATABASE BEFORE PERFORMING A RESTORATION FROM THE BACKUPS.

THE DEFAULT SETTING IS THAT THE MONGOSTORE WILL ESTABLISH A CONNECTION TO AN INSTANCE OF MONGODB WHICH IS EXECUTING ON THE LOCALHOST INTERFACE, THAT IS, 127.0.0.1 AND THE DEFAULT PORT WHICH IS 27017. FOR THE RESTORATION TO BE DONE IN A DIFFERENT HOST OR PORT, THEN THE OPTIONS "—HOST" AND "—PORT" CAN BE USED. CONSIDER THE EXAMPLE GIVEN BELOW:

mongorestore --host mongodb1.mydb.net --port 3017 --username user --password pass /opt/backup/mongodump-2013-10-24

In case authentication with the MongoDB is needed, you have to specify both the username and the password for your database. This has been shown in the example given above.

Import/Export

The tools mongoimport and mongoexport which are used in MongoDB assist in working with the data which is in a human-readable format, which is either CSV or Extended JSON format. If the data migration, either export or import, is complex, you might need to come up with your own import and export scripts which you will use together with the client driver so as to interact with your database.

The commands copydb, clone, or cloneCollection can be used for the purpose of copying a database from one instance to another, and they may be more suitable for certain tasks than others. When using the mongo shell, you will be provided with the method "*db.copyDatabase()*."

When exporting in the CSV format, the fields of the documents to export to have to be specified. This involves specifying the "*name*" and the "*address*" fields to export. This is shown below:

**mongoexport --db users --collection contacts --
type=csv --fields name,address --out
/opt/backups/contacts.csv**

In this case, the fields can also be specified in a file having a list of fields separated by lines. These should be the fields which are to be exported.

A good example is the *"name"* and *"address"* fields which can be specified in the file *"fileds.txt."* These are shown below:

name

address

You should then use the option *"—fieldFile"* so as to specify the fields which are to be exported within the file. This is shown below:

**mongoexport --db users --collection contacts --
type=csv --fieldFile fields.txt --out
/opt/backups/contacts.csv**

Conclusion

It can be concluded that MongoDB is a very powerful NoSQL database which is in use today. With MongoDB, both the software developers and database developers can perform numerous operations, ranging from the simple to the complex ones. That is how powerful the database is. It provides them with automatic scaling, good performance, and high availability. This means that the user will experience the ease of use when working with MongoDB.

The number of records or documents which can be supported by this database is also large. Most of the operations in MongoDB are based on replica sets. The operations are usually carried out on these replica sets. A replica set has a number of users, and one can feel free to create and add users to it. The users can also be deleted from the replica set or the information about them updated. This book has explored all of these processes and you have learned how they can be done.

The data stored in the data files can also be backed up so as to cater to the circumstances under which failures occur. There are various ways that one can perform a backup of their database in MongoDB. This book has discussed some of these ways.

Once you have performed a backup of your data and then a failure occurs, such as an unexpected shutdown of your database, you will have to perform a recovery of your database. The data files are always left in an inconsistent state once errors have occurred, such as an unexpected shutdown. To bring it back to a consistent state, you have to perform a recovery of the data. This book guides you on how to do this.

www.ingramcontent.com/pod-product-compliance
Lightning Source LLC
Chambersburg PA
CBHW071552080326
40690CB00056B/1797